The Art of Teaching

What They Didn't Tell You in College

First Edition, Soft Cover

Copyright 2011
By Eric Gibbons

ISBN - 10: 1456497669
ISBN - 13: 978-1456497668

Printer: Createspace

Additional copies may be ordered direct from the publisher at a substantial discount. Please contact LOVSART@gmail.com for additional information. Subject line: The Art of Teaching. Signed and inscribed editions are also available via the same email address.

Thank You to the following contributors to this book:
Joshua Kavett, Penny Kearns, Kathy Potts, Michelle Lovejoy, Robert Platt, Amelia Tahaney

Cover Model: Kimberlyann Michelson

The ART of Teaching—Introduction
By Eric Gibbons

What They Didn't Tell You in College

Often, teaching can be a whole different experience than what prospective educators have been told in college. This book provides "Real Life" experience from a teacher with 20+ years in the trenches and his colleagues.

Teaching is NOT for everyone. It takes a special person with a lot of patience and organization to teach. Procrastinators will find themselves underwater in short order as well as in violation of the LAW in some cases.

Teachers are scrutinized with background checks, finger printing and are on file with the FBI. Though *Freedom of Speech* is in our Constitution, there are some very real limits about what a teacher can and cannot say in the classroom or even outside the school or on the internet. These constraints may simply be too much for some.

You will never be paid what your work is actually worth or the hours you really put in, and the politics of unions, parents, and administration can sour your enthusiasm. In many places, the whole profession of teaching is under attack as an easy/soft target to squeeze financially by cutting benefits and salaries.

That said, the rewards are numerous as well. I make a comfortable middle-class salary. I still have students visiting me many years after graduation thanking me for my influence in their lives. I know I have saved several from the brink of suicide with the help of a guidance counselor; I have championed students who would otherwise be lost in the system, I have planted the seeds of my own content expertise and have witnessed the blossoming and growth in my students firsthand. I have affected lives for the better and some have become lifelong friends. Though I love my subject, it is because of some of these less tangible reasons why I am a teacher.

Content Topics:

Overview

Classroom Management

Getting Set Up

Student Issues

Getting and Keeping Your Job

74. The Reality of Tenure and Non-tenure
75. A Teaching Portfolio (Createspace.com)
76. Resume That Looks Like Your Content Area
77. Parents as Advocates (Letters of Recommendation)
77. How Soon Administrators Should Know Your Name
78. Unions and Contracts
79. Promote, Promote, Promote
80. Personal Development and Continuing Education
80. Use Technology

Personal Issues

81. $aving for Retirement and Investing ASAP
82. Find Your Passion Outside School to Avoid Burn-out
82. Keeping School Drama Out of Your Home
83. Dating at Work/"Frenemies"
84. Discrimination and Issues at work

98. Something for Art Teachers

Top 10 Qualities of a Great Teacher

1 Patience
2 Consistency
3 Professionalism
4 Organization
5 Communication dexterity
6 Ability to ask for help
7 Think on your feet
8 Emotional Detachment
9 Seeks Professional Growth
10 Love your subject!

1 Patience: Remember, kids are kids.

This seems simple enough, but easy to forget. There are real differences in the child's brain from early years through the teen years. Kids are sometimes irrational, undependable, secretive, distrustful, lazy, and inappropriate. Sometimes when we see this behavior we lose our cool and think they are doing it "on purpose."

This is going to seem politically incorrect, but it's the best way I can put it—I see my students as mentally disabled with moments of clarity. On some cognitive level this is true because they are still developing. Would I get angry if a child with Down Syndrome did something wrong? No. I would take their disability into consideration and moderate my tone and approach.

If we see that kids are simply not fully developed people—works in progress—it can take the sting out of poor behavior. Instead of getting angry, think of their disability and react without anger or spite.

2 Consistency: No favoritism.

You will like some students more than others. We do not like to say this, but it is obvious. Also, a child you have difficulty with may be the "teacher's pet" in another room. The point is not to base your classroom management on how you feel about your students but on your classroom rules. If the "good kid" steps out of line, then he or she should receive the same consequences as that kid you have difficulty with so that all can see and understand you are fair and consistent. If a child breaks school policies, that student should be dealt with in the same way.

3 Professionalism: Keep your personal life private.

Though it is fine to be friendly to students, it is important that you not cross the line to become a friend. You are the instructor and need to remain the authority figure. There is no need to "dominate" the class, but sharing too much information, certainly personal information, can be problematic, especially in this age of the internet.

In many schools, teachers are forbidden to have a Facebook or Twitter page. Other schools encourage it but have strict guideline about the usage. My personal feeling is that you should not connect with students through any means outside of school, via the internet or in person. There are simply too many lawsuits that point to the errors of such behavior. Even innocent communication can be taken out of context and be used against you. EVERYTHING you email or post on the internet is permanently recorded. Though you hit delete, the information is still obtainable by authorities.

Students, by their very nature are inconsistent. You can be their best friend one day and the next, they hate you and want to do everything they can to punish you. Imagine a "good student" who rightfully earns a detention, their feelings can change on a dime and you are the one leaving yourself vulnerable.

This is not meant to alarm you, but social interactions of any kind put you in a very bad position and open to legal issues far deeper than you would like to explore. You need to care. You need to connect. You need to share, but do so as a professional.

4 Organization: Paperwork and the legal things you must do.

The paperwork outside the classroom can be overwhelming. Then you add in all the work that pertains to your subject and there is a mountain that needs to be climbed on a daily basis. The documentation escalates and seems to have no end, but if you are organized and do it as it come up, you can stay above the rising waters. Getting behind too can put you in violation of the law.

Some students have special accommodations you are legally bound to have available and follow at all times. Never mind that you teach 150 students a day; you have to make concrete accommodations for these students and it is NOT always easy. There could be a spot inspection by state authorities and if that paperwork is not available, you can lose your teaching certificate. It is that serious. It is also difficult to meet all expectations. For example, you may have 5 students who need special seating for fewer distractions. Every classroom only four corners; what are you to do?

Attendance too is a major consideration. There are laws that speak to this in each state, but essentially if a student's attendance is erroneously recorded and he is hurt or does something irrational (like pulling a fire alarm) while not accounted for, YOU may be partially liable for not following procedure. Attendance can be one of the little things that slip in a classroom, but the ramifications can be enormous.

Then there are issues of lesson plans, formative and summative assessments, documentation, curriculum, mandated testing, in-service work, and other paperwork generated by the office; all of these can lead to negative reports added to your personnel file and be the reason you are denied an annual increment or are outright fired. Though tenure gives you some protection, any school can fire any teacher who does not follow procedures. Tenure just means they have to prove that you are ineffective.

5 Communication dexterity: Kids, parents, colleagues, administrators...

As a teacher you are confronted by diverse populations all with different expectations of your role as a teacher. You must be able to speak clearly to each in the most professional way possible because your interactions can have a dramatic effect on your job and even your working conditions.

- Communicate poorly to students, they don't succeed, and you are labeled a bad teacher.
- Communicate poorly to parents and you will get complaints to your supervisor.
- Communicate poorly to your colleagues and you are isolated
- Communicate poorly to administrators and it can affect your working conditions or employment.

6 Ability to ask for help.

Though you should be capable of teaching alone and seek help on your own, collaboration and communication with other teachers can be a huge benefit. If you wait too long to ask for help, you can find yourself too far behind to recover. By seeking out colleagues, you can learn from their successes, empathize about the problems you share, solve problems together, and seek the help of veteran teachers and administrators. NEVER feel that asking for help makes you appear to be a poor teacher. Some of the best teachers I know collaborate often. Ask a colleague to observe your class informally for suggestions; a new point of view can be invaluable!

Islands can be pretty, but they can also be very lonely places.

7 Think on your feet: Change lessons on a spur moment.

Though it is important to follow curriculum and be consistent, you are not a robot, and sometimes things come up that are both pertinent and relevant. You may find a way to refocus a lesson that will grab students' attention. When you do this they see that their input matters.

Some tangents can be negative and some positive. Take a moment and think it through. These are golden opportunities, though admittedly some will just be distractions. You need to remain alert to these possibilities and "roll with it" and use that flexibility to excite your students.

Another aspect of this is that "S**T happens." The internet can be down, power outages happen, kids don't bring in supplies you assigned for homework (like bring in a magazine, etc.) So you must be able to find an alternate path to switch gears and move on. Thinking on your feet is just part of the job. Have a fun lesson stashed away for such an occasion.

8 Emotional Detachment: Don't take everything personally, Think it through.

Similar in thought to number one, you need to have a clinical detachment to the emotional drama of school and see it for what it is. This does not mean you need to be cold and detached, but it does mean you need to see the behavior and situation for what it is. Students are under-developed adults. If you attribute adult willfulness to their behavior you will only become frustrated. Students often have a narrow range of reactions to situations. They do not think of the larger implication to their behavior and they lack experiences to teach them these things in a meaningful way.

As a teacher, you are often the one to help them understand these things. You need to show them the options and let them choose. And you need to enforce the outcomes. You are the police, judge, jury, lawyer, and policy maker. You need to expect that issues will arise daily. Most will be small, but as these experiences accumulate, the student forms the foundation for their own adult behavior. Arbitrary enforcement only reinforces the idea that consequences are arbitrary as well.

One indication that you have an issue here is by calculating how often you feel the need to raise your voice. If it is daily, then you have a problem. Yelling means that you have lost your cool, the students have the upper hand, and you were unable to detach yourself from the behavior. Do you like to be yelled at? I would assume not.

Challenge yourself not to yell. I did it for a year and much of what I learned and share with you here is rooted in this one simple yet profound challenge. When students act out, I remind them of my expectation or posted rules. I will issue a warning and follow through if they do not comply. Sometimes it means sending them to the office to "cool off" without a detention, sometimes with. I escalate the consequences little by little until they comply. If you hit them with a sledgehammer for the first infraction, they will see you as arbitrary and an ogre they cannot respect and their behavior will get worse. Later in this book I will share with you my approach to disciplinary problems.

9 Seeks Professional Growth: Stay current.

I have learned very little from in-school professional growth, though a few things stand out: Information about laws that effect our profession, health issues to be aware of, and suicide prevention, but this is a sliver of the nearly 100 programs I have attended.

The most valuable growth comes when I have been able to meet with colleagues within my subject area and participate in collaborative workshops where we share best practices, lesson ideas, share suggestions, and meet the vendors that supply our department. These often happen at conventions, either state or national, and I would encourage teachers to attend these.

Professional development need not be confined to these areas; you may consider an evening class or two within or related to your subject. The additional classes may help you accrue credit to ascend faster on your school's salary guide. Many schools will often reimburse part of your tuition based on the grades you receive.

10 Love what you teach!

Your own feelings of personal well-being have a direct effect on your students. If you teach a subject you do not have a passion about, maybe you should consider a change of subject or career. Students are like little emotional tuning-forks, they can sense if you are "phoning it in" or if your interest is genuine. Your enthusiasm should be contagious.

How does one stay interested and not "burn out" For some, taking their subject outside the classroom is beneficial, easily understood when you think of an art teacher painting and exhibiting. A colleague friend of mine teaches math and tells me that the last thing he wants to do is more math when he gets home. Instead he finds that golf and gardening keep him fresh. You may find a woodworking class for a science teacher may simply allow for creative energies to express themselves and make for a happier person. Some find their bliss in daily work-out routines, quilting, scrapbooking, painting, and exhibiting.

It is especially important that teachers stay fresh and refreshed. Teaching is extremely taxing. I would challenge any hedge-fund-millionaire to do one week in a classroom successfully. Teaching is not for everyone, but at a minimum, you must love what you teach.

Does the FBI Think Are You Fit to be a Teacher?

Every teacher and many other school employees must submit to fingerprinting and agree to a background check so that they are on file with the FBI. You may also be required to pass a blood or screen test to rule out illicit drug use.

If you were a casual marijuana user in college, this behavior will prevent you from being hired and will probably be on file somewhere depending on how far into the application process you have gone. If you have a criminal background, you will be unable to teach. This would not include traffic tickets, just criminal activity and convictions.

If you lie on any of your applications or embellish your resume, you can easily be dismissed. It is very important to be as honest and candid as possible in all regards to the hiring process.

The Relevant Lesson: No One Likes too Many Vegetables

The most successful educators I have ever known have had one thing in common: They tie their lessons into the students' experiences and lives to make their subject relevant. This avoids the all too common question: "When are we ever gonna' have to know this stuff?!" When subject matter relates to the student, they are motivated and want to learn. If you love your subject, that enthusiasm too will also be contagious.

This is easier to say than do and will take some creativity on your part. You need to marry your specific curriculum to the textbook and then to the student experience. Find out what interests students and work out ways to incorporate that into the lesson units. You may find that a survey at the beginning and end of the year will be helpful. Find out what they want to know about within your subject, and even what they don't care about. This may reveal things you were unaware of. An exit survey may help you fine tune what you are doing. Find out what they liked most and least. Even ask for suggestions.

Check too with colleagues. They may have awesome lessons to share with you and there may be some good information on the internet.

Some examples:
- Art students can create a mobile based on symbolic representation of members of their family.
- Math students can research the salary guides of their chosen career path or of someone they admire and complete math problems accordingly; tax rates, percentages of expenses over net salary etc.
- World language students can make translations of their own writings.

Substitute Teaching and Substitute Teachers: 2 sides to the coin.

Substitute teaching may be a great way to get your foot in the door. In most places you can begin as a junior in college with 60 college credits. You will have to go through the background check and fingerprinting, but the advantages may outweigh the inconvenience. Pay is modest, and there are often more subs available than any school actually needs. If you are called in, do your best to impress. When a teacher returns and finds that their students actually completed work and did it well, they can often ask the sub coordinator to request you again. I have. I know others who have too. Your name will be recognizable and that may give you a serious edge if a position opens up.

Always follow written lesson plans. Leave brief but pertinent notes about what you completed, questions students may have had. Note the behavior of the class as a whole, as well as pointing out anyone who gave you some difficulty.

DO NOT make up your own lessons unless nothing is left for you. DO NOT criticize the practices of the teacher you are substituting for, it will only reflect badly on you. If students like you, encourage them to speak to their teacher about how much they enjoyed having you there.

More often than not, days that a substitute is in are days that are lost. With that in mind, I have a library of videos ready for these days that cover historical information about my content area. Students have to complete a video notes worksheet to show evidence that they were paying attention and it is graded— though mainly based on completeness. It is factored into their homework grade comprising 10% of their final grade. I can count on being absent about 6 days a year on average and these lessons are ready at a moment's notice.

Many districts require emergency lesson plans, but if not, these should be available at all times in a place they cannot be lost along with notes about specific health alerts a sub should know about. (like a student who is epileptic)

Generally you need to be prepared for the worst but praise the sub who does well for you. A note to administration will be appreciated and good coverage should be noted and rewarded if possible.

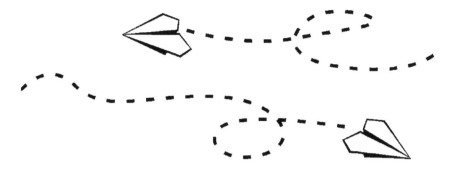

Classroom Management

Be Real to Engage Students

How does one **not** "be real"? By talking down to or at students, by not staying current with their interests, by loosing your cool, or being too "cold."

This is a real balancing act and at first may seem to conflict with #8 to be emotionally detached. If you address students as if they were people like yourself, it may be helpful in letting them sympathize with you and vise-versa. Ask yourself, how would you like to be spoken to? How would you like your supervisor to react to your mistakes or misunderstandings? How would you expect your colleague to approach you if they had a problem with something you did? By treating students with the same respect you demand of others, you will earn their respect and you will be giving them a living example to help form their own patterns of behavior.

If you go into teaching thinking that you are only here to teach your content area, you will be very frustrated and disappointed. Much of what teaching is, is modeling and teaching appropriate behavior. I am often still surprised by student behavior—like at a concert where students continue to chat while others are singing for them. They need to be told what one should and should not do at a concert/theatre. Sometimes you need to make connections for them. You can say, "This is like going to church or a movie, you need to remain quiet for the performer." Additionally you should connect with their emotional side by adding something like "Imagine if you were on stage and worked for months to prepare for this presentation but people talked over you. How would that make you feel?"

This last part is where you will find the most effective use of communication to change behavior. Children are emotional people. They react often based on their feelings without considering the possible ramifications of that behavior. It's also why we do not apply the death sentence to smaller children as they have less capacity to understand fully the consequences of their behavior. There is evidence that the human brain does not fully develop these abilities until the age of about 25.

Understanding this lack of development can help you remain calm when these issues arise. It is simply the nature of children, not a willful negligence or ignorance. It should not surprise you that this behavior does not disappear after one incident. Appropriate behavior needs to be modeled again and again, and if the consequences or reactions to such behavior is consistent, learning takes place.

Let's take the example of my student teacher "C.R." Two boys in class were having an inappropriate conversation of a sexual nature. She rightly addressed it and told them to stop. She had to do so a few times and noted that the behavior was inappropriate.

My advice to her was to take the students into the hallway and personalize their behavior. I told her to say to them, "Guys, I know you're just joking around, but when you speak like that it makes me feel uncomfortable as a woman. I am sure that was not what you meant to do, but it is how I feel. Also, as a teacher I need to be sure all my students are comfortable too. If I feel this way, I am sure others do too but they can't really say anything or kids will make fun of them for being uptight. If one of them complained, I'd be called down to the office and asked to explain why I let this behavior continue and they would see me as a bad teacher. Could you guys change the topic? I want you to have fun and enjoy my class, but this really has to stop."

By personalizing the behavior they now understand how you feel. (Even if you have to exaggerate a bit about how you really feel.) Making a concrete example helps them understand the feelings of the situation so it will resonate with them. They will also know you care because you took the time to explain it and didn't just yell at them and say "knock it off." You may argue that this exchange will take too much time out of your class, but consider that this approach may stop this behavior immediately and prevent it from re-occurring. If you add up all your "knock it off" distractions, I think in the long term you will be saving time. Students who see you address these issues privately in the hall will feel more at ease that you care enough to explain things, that you did not yell, that you remained calm, and that you can be trusted.

This takes practice but works for the behavior you really need to shut down before it can potentially escalate. Keep in mind too that if you don't address some behaviors, like teasing, you can be in violation of Title 9 Federal Law.

Yelling is YOUR Problem, Not Theirs.

There are only 2 issues where I raise my voice.
- Safety issues (Kids playing with a sharp object)
- Bullying

About five years into teaching I found myself "burning out" and getting upset with the behavior of my students. I was giving several detentions daily, often raising my voice and was on the verge of cursing on a couple occasions. Though I would never condone a teacher "losing it" in the classroom, I can definitely understand how it can happen.

I felt I could not sustain the kind of energy I was expending on a daily basis. Though I am not sure where the idea came from, I know I chose to complete that year by doing all I could to not raise my voice. This was in the fall, so I knew it would be a challenge. I would do everything I could to avoid it and that forced me to change my approach and leads to much that is contained herein.

One thing I did was I began to sit with my students as they worked and learn a bit about what they were doing and thinking, thereby making some valuable one-on-one connections.

Then I remembered the thing about "I" statements from a therapy class I took in college. That an "I" statement helps deflate situations and that "You" statements tend to exacerbate them. For instance: "Why can't you stay in your seat!" verses "Tommy, I would really appreciate it if you would remain in your seat." The tonal difference is clear but it is also clear that the "I" statement may feel unnatural or alien. This does take practice.

If the behavior continues, then another more detailed connection needs to be made. This will take a bit of thought and practice. "Tommy, I can see you really have a lot of energy and it is difficult to stay in your seat. I know it may seem silly to have to do it, but when you walk around it is distracting to the students and even I have a hard time concentrating because I am worrying about what you are going to do. I also worry that maybe I am not being a good teacher because I can't seem to help you listen. What can we do together to make this better?" After considering seat changes, and all the normal approaches to this behavior, think about a reward for sitting, maybe a little private extra credit, every day in the seat is an additional point on the next test? You really need to stretch your creative muscles to make this work but it can be done and the result is that the student now sympathizes, their behavior becomes more compliant, and they are more likely to listen to your directions in the future because they feel you care.

All students and you will benefit from rewarding good behavior and praise now and again. During your class closure, you can make a statement about the overall behavior when it is good. Pass little notes to students who are usually troublesome that say, "Thank you for staying in your seat, I really appreciate it!" Little notes like these are like little surprises. Maybe stock up on little "thank you" stationary from the Dollar Store. You can even slip in a little chocolate or some fun stickers.

The big idea here is to speak to kids as you would like to be spoken to and reward good behavior as often, or MORE often than you address bad behavior.

If you find you are unable to keep your cool, or that a particular student very easily "pushes your buttons," look within. There is an interesting psychological term called counter-transference. Simply put, it is when you react to others unknowingly because they express feelings and emotions you suppress in yourself. Review your interactions to be sure this is not part of them.

If the "needy" kid gets on your nerves, look to your own "neediness" and see if there is some truth to this and possibly the root of your losing your cool. Often identifying the root issue can solve the problem.

In Like a Lion, Out Like a Lamb

One of the great "Truths" about teaching is it is easier to come on strong and losen up later. Displaying your rules in the bulletin board can be an effective reminder of your expectations.

It is always difficult to crack down on bad behavior that you have let escalate. If you set a tone of control, organization, and consistency from day one, it is easier to nip these bad behaviors early. As the year progresses their behavior will be more controlled. As it does, you can losen the constraints a bit. This does not mean to become lax; but seating assignments can change, maybe music can be played during individual work-time. It can take the form you feel a more "relaxed" situation should be with you in charge.

The beginning of the year is the time to set strict rules and follow through on consequences. It is your time to learn about the individual needs of your students and build relationships. It is your time to find out what motivates them.

Don't be a "Friend," be a Teacher; Being Fair vs Being Liked

If one of your goals is that you are "liked" by students, you have a long and painful road ahead.

If you are fair, consistent, and respectful of your students, students will like you, but it should never be a goal. Your primary goal is to teach your subject matter and manage your room. It is what you are paid to do and there is nobility in this profession of education.

Personally, I would much more appreciate that my students respect me than like me.

As teachers, we see unmanageable students from time to time, with parents that have no sympathy or respect for what we do. Some joke that "The apple doesn't fall far from the tree," but my own experience is that many of these issues stem from "Friendship Parenting." Most parents do not receive the training we do about behavior modification, positive reinforcement, and enforcing consequences for choices. They may not have come out of good family situations themselves.

These are the parents that base their discipline on how their children will feel about their parenting. They are afraid they will come off as mean. They want their kids to be their friends, so they are overly lenient and do not set clear boundaries nor do they follow-through in a consistent way with consequences. This sets up a pattern of confusion as expectations cannot be gauged.

These are the parents that agree with their child when a student says, "Mr. So-and-so hates me!" They call, they yell, they assume you are out to "get their child," when all you are doing is being clear about expectations and holding them to the boundaries you have set. In these cases you should make your supervisor aware of these communications. If they are sent via email, send a copy of all correspondence to your director as well. Do not be an island, especially if you do not have tenure.

Get Off Your Butt and Sit with the Kids.

At the same time I decided to try not yelling for a year, I also made up a chart and was deliberate in my attempt to sit with each student for a short time while they worked on projects. I used this time to learn a bit about them and their interests and even how they were feeling about the class. These conversations, still today, give me ideas for projects.

Building these mini students-teacher relationships will help lessen the confrontations in your room and help students know, in a real way, that you do care. It is important to see all of them with equal attentiveness. Students are keenly aware if you are "faking it" and that your interest is less than genuine.

You have nothing to lose and everything to gain by making these important connections.

Detentions and Blaming the Boss.

Make sure you follow your school's procedures for detentions. Every school will be different.

I generally give detentions as per issues of breaking school rules. I am supposed to assign them for a student's fourth tardy to class, if I catch them cutting class, texting on cell phones, if they plagiarize an assignment, etc. For some of these issues I "blame the boss." I tell my student this: "I am hired by the school to enforce the rules. I may not like all the rules much myself, but that's part of what they pay me to do. If I do not give you the detention for the fourth tardy, they can see my attendance, and they can look for the detention receipt. If there is no receipt then I am in violation of my contract and I get called to the principal's office. Just as you have to follow the rules, I do too. There are consequences for me if I do not follow the rules. I could get fired. This is not personal. I do not think you are a bad person; it's just that I have to assign this detention."

This seems like an awful lot to say but it does deflate the situation. It now becomes a non-emotional issue, you have spoken to the child as an adult, you have outlined the deeper issues behind the detention, and they may understand it is not a personal issue.

The other reason I give detentions is the bullying issues or safety in the classroom. Often in these cases I speak to the student in the hallway without their peers. I give them a long "I" statement explanation of the situation and give them some options: Cool off in the office or nurse, separation from the problem, a chance to apologize, or whatever else may fit the issue. Sometimes this is enough. Sometimes it is not. The main thing is to be consistent whether the student is a "good" or "problem" child.

Dress Code Violations and Your Dress Code

Every school is different in regard to this one. The dress code may be very different from Georgia to Minnesota if not simply for the temperature differences. There are pitfalls to avoid that can put you in difficult situations.

As a male teacher, I alert the office as to a female student's dress-code violation. I would never confront them about it as it may put me in the position of responding to "Hey, why are you paying attention to what I am wearing?" I just opt-out and pass the buck. For male students I can just tell them to go and change a shirt or whatever. Often nurses' offices will have extra items students can wear. Some schools make the kids wear an oversized shirt that covers everything. I have heard rumors about some of these shirts being silkscreened, "I was in violation of the Dress Code." As cute as that may be, it may actually be in violation of the law as it singles them out and exposes them to possible ridicule among their peers. (I smell a lawsuit waiting to happen.)

Think too of the example you set as well. Choose clothing that is professional and appropriate for your job. A shop teacher will dress differently from a history teacher for safety reasons. (You wouldn't want a tie to get caught in a band-saw) Some schools may even have a strict dress code anyway.

Ladies need to consider their dress too. Try to wear items that will not be distracting to teenage boys. Though this may sound silly, I have seen this happen and shake my head wondering where common sense has gone. Spaghetti-strapped or short-cut anything is really not appropriate in any school, no matter how hot or humid.

New teachers may only be a few years older than their high school students and how you dress will help separate you from them in a visual way. If you dress like them, you may lose your authoritative edge.

"Engage" the Thugs

This heading may not be all that "Politically Correct," but there is truth in it.

If at all possible, I try to engage the most difficult students early in the year. I give them a few additional responsibilities, and give them a bit more positive reinforcement so they may be more likely "on my side." There is a careful balance here though. You do not want them to be your friends, but you certainly do not want them to be your enemies. If you over do it, others in the room will label it as favoritism. If you give them a bit of lenience, do it on the side and away from others, just be sure they must be as responsible as the others in what is expected.

I think of this as healthy pro-active classroom maintenance. In many instances your classroom can hinge on these few but powerful personalities. They are looked up to for their independence and if they think you are "cool" the rest of the class may follow. I know for certain that when some personalities are absent for sickness the whole tone of the classroom can be completely different. This only illustrates why you may need to get them on your side if possible.

It is however, not always possible and then you are left to just "deal with it." When this happens, just be very clear about your expectations and very clear about the consequences.

Some simple things you can do are find out their interests and see if you can draw parallels to your own life. Share a bit. Consider going to see movies you hear them talk about. It may not be your "thing" but it will educate you about their world and may help you create lessons that connect with their experiences. Also, by seeing what they see, you will be more clued into their "lingo." What may be considered a compliment, may, in the context of a popular video, actually be an insult. Do you know what it means if a kid yells "Bob Sagett?" I do and only because I catch up on YouTube quite often.

Getting Set Up

Seating Charts and Assigned Seats (And Adjustments)

For those free thinkers among us, assigned seats might be a four letter word. I have tried both and invariably assigned seats have always helped classroom management. It also means you can learn student names a bit faster. You can collect and pass out work more efficiently, and attendance is less likely to be incorrect. (Remember that attendance is a legal issue as well.)

When students choose for themselves, they sit with friends and are far more interested in socialization than your content area. I do however allow for some adjustment at the end of the first quarter IF the class is well behaved. This can be an optional motivating factor, a privilege that can be taken back based on their own behavior.

You will also need to monitor classroom dynamics. Some kids simply have difficulty being near others because of past drama. If you spot something that causes you concern, ask about it, check out the reality of the situation, and then address it.

Personally, I group my students because about 20% to 30% of my projects are group work. I cover my seating charts with projector/overhead plastic and write on it with Sharpie marker. I clean it daily with rubbing alcohol. I can make notes, take grades, and everything is there and then enter it on the computer when I am able. This is really helpful if power goes out or the computers are not working properly.

Whenever you get stuck for ideas, ask your fellow teachers or simply observe what they do.

Homeroom and Attendance

As I said earlier, there are laws that speak to this in each state, but essentially if a student's attendance is erroneously recorded and he is hurt or does something irrational (like pulling a fire alarm) while not accounted for,) YOU may be partially liable for not following procedure. Attendance can be one of the little things that slip in a classroom, but the ramifications can be enormous. Though tenure gives you some protection, any school can fire any teacher who does not follow procedures.

This is most critical in homeroom. Some schools conduct homeroom within the first period class. Either way, the first attendance of the day is the most important. Parents are usually alerted shortly thereafter, they need to know if their child is not where he or she needs to be. Though mistakes happen, these are the least forgivable and can have the largest effect on your employment. Take the time during homeroom to be as accurate as possible.

Documenting attendance throughout the day is as important. The school rush can make attendance difficult, but authorities don't want to hear excuses. I generally double-check my attendance at the end of the period to be sure a kid didn't slip in or out during my class.

If you have passes for the lavatory or other areas, it is important that students sign in or out. there have been numerous times I have had to refer to these papers when issues happen in school. If you mark a kid absent but they were in the bathroom (happens often) then you have back-up documentation. I also call out, "I have the following kids absent today, if you are here, speak up..."

This documentation too is helpful when a student's grade is in danger. Your good record keeping will show if they have been in class and if they were out for long periods. If a student is absent for a long period of time I like to check and be sure they really are absent or just skipping my class.

I had a really great "scammer" come to me with a sign out sheet. He told me he was transferring to another school. He copied a form from another student who was transferring and lied to me. He didn't come for about 2 weeks and I saw him again in the hallway. It turns out he was spending my period in lunch with his buddies. I had the documentation and contacted the administration as soon as I found out. My clue was that his name did not disappear from my attendance.

Always double check these things; don't assume that you are always being told the truth. Ultimately it falls on your head if there is an issue. YOU are the responsible adult, so request documentation and check up on it.

Pass Points

I have created 4 coupons students keep in their folders called "Pass Points." They get only 4 for the year and I counter sign them in color marker. One can be used in lieu of missing homework, or for a day they do not participate, or need to do other work. I request a Pass Point if they have chosen not to participate as well or assess a zero for that day. We all have issues that come up, so this allows them the freedom to make an adult choice. They cannot use Pass Points on days I am testing or giving important notes though.

Students can also use Pass Points to add 10 points to any quiz, test, or exam. I tell them they can save them up, get a 60% on the final and use all 4 to make it a 100%. The point is that by participating always, they bank these points. I have found that it does improve overall participation.

A+ B- C+ F A-

Grades

As much as possible, it is important to be able to defend the grades you give. You need to remove arbitrary assessments from the mix. Often a rubric is the best way to break down a grade. I like to have a side-by-side form where students grade themselves first and then I grade them. They know only my grade counts. The point however is that if they give themselves an "A" for completeness and I give them a "C" for it, we can have a discussion about what completeness means for me. As the year progresses they will better meet your expectations and the grades will be more and more similar. Once that has been established, if grades are different, you can have a short conversation about it and maybe they can enlighten you too about their own process, which may help you redefine your lessons or understand your student's comprehension.

This will be helpful when parents approach you about the grades their children have received. You should have this back-up assessment information on hand.

I generally include a synopsis of how the grade is assessed in my online grade book that is accessible by parents via the internet. By doing this I find that there are less questions and parents, when seeing their child's project, can see if it meets these expectations.

I do grade for participation. I give every student 100% to start with and then deduct up to 10 points for non-participation. When a student chooses not to participate, I deduct some points and let them know. If they completely refuse to work, it might be the full 10 points. This is an opportunity to check if everything is OK with that student. Sometimes nonparticipation can be a clue to larger issues.

As I stated before, students are highly emotional beings, so their feelings often determine what they do and choose not to do. You need to investigate changes in behavior if their nonparticipation is unusual. It can be an indication of drug issues, stress, bereavement, pre-suicidal issues, and more.

Tests, Exams and Assessments (Accommodations)

It is always important to have differentiated assessments. In short, be sure to have a variety of way to assess your students throughout the year. These can be given orally, via tests, projects, presentations, written reports, quizzes of different styles, and even non-graded assessments can be helpful in understanding your children's levels of understanding.

If all of your tests are fill-in-the-blank or multiple choice, you are only getting assessments based on the kids who do and do not do that well. It may not be a fair assessment of knowledge. ALSO you may not be meeting the guidelines of the accommodations required for your special needs students (504 plan or I.E.P.) If you are not in compliance, then you put your teaching certificate in jeopardy.

I sometimes make 2 versions of my tests, so students can choose the version at whichthey feel they will be most successful. I tell them a "little white lie" that the tests are different, but they are often not, they just look different. This makes it easier for me to grade later. Most never notice.

On one occasion, because of snow-days, I had to give a short test. I didn't get copies yet, so I gave them the same review sheet, and only a very small handful of students even said anything. Sadly, there were a handful that failed the test, even though the it was the same thing they recently completed.

It can be frustrating.

I also speak one-on-one with my special needs students and their guidance representative and see if it would be helpful for them to test with their guidance person. This has been very helpful and offers another layer of proof that you are in compliance of state and federal accommodations.

Paperwork

The daily load of paperwork can be overwhelming. My best advice here is to do it as soon as possible. This can make me a bit of a hermit. I do all I can to be sure I take as little home as possible. I use my preparation period and resource period to do this work. It means I have a bit less time with colleagues, but it also means that often, at the end of the day, it is truly the end of my day. Conversely it also means I really need a nap once I get home.

This may simply be impossible for some subject areas and it may take some creativity to figure out how to leave work at work. This is also why you will never be paid for the hours you truly work. Though I try to do it all at work, the truth is that sometimes there are truly not enough hours in the day.

If however you find that you are spending more than 5 hours weekly at home doing school work, it may be a good idea to check with colleagues if they are having the same experience. If not, find out what they do to reduce their workload. You might find some great and helpful ideas!

Lesson Plans – Every School is Different

Some schools require daily plans, others weekly, and some just unit overviews. Ultimately what matters is what is in your contract. You need to meet those requirements and deadlines. Because non-compliance can get you fired, I am sure to upload lessons early, generally about 3 days before I need to so if I need to make an adjustment, I can.

Look up Bloom's Taxonomy for good "power words" to include in your lesson plans. I like to use this website: www.officeport.com/edu/blooms.htm. These are the key words administrators like to see. They also like to see evidence of backward design (students working to a known goal, art teachers do it naturally) and "big questions" or understandings. These are the overall "things" all your students should learn within the current lesson.

These are OVERLY simplified and whole books are written on these topics and more. Every district has its set of buzzwords and goals. You need to stay focused on what your own district requires.

Fire Alarms and Alerts

I can't imagine a school that does not have a plan of action available to all teachers. With all the fire drills we do and emergency evacuations twice monthly, there must be a plan and you need to know it. You also need to know what to do if you do not have kids at that time. You need to be sure your subs have this information; most districts let them know it. If your school does not have a good plan of action, you should bring it to their attention via email so there is evidence that it was a concern, and that you expressed it. Email is becoming more and more important in legal cases as it is easy to trace and difficult to alter and falsify.

With every class, you need to review the evacuation route from your room. It may be different for every room a child visits. You will also need to know how your population will react to an alarm. If you have an autistic child or someone with a seizure disorder, an alarm can sometimes set them off. You need to be prepared for these possible eventualities.

It is important to review your attendance once you have evacuated to be sure you have all the students you should. This is required (or should be) of all districts. You need to report irregularities as soon as possible to avoid liability. Even if you think you know where your student is when they are not with you, it is prudent to note it. What if the child you think is in the library was the one that pulled a false alarm? You may be brought into the office and questioned about any inconsistencies.

37

Don't Call From Home or Use Personal Email

Try as best you can to keep school business on school property. It is important for liability reasons not to engage parents, students, and administrators in a social context. I would include teachers that are not close personal friends in this list. I feel it's fine to be friendly and sociable, but be professional as well.

Calling parents from your home means they can call you back on your time. (Caller I.D.) Emailing people from your personal account means that ALL your life, outside of school, can be tapped into. Every blog, every post, every personal ad you have ever had connected to your personal email can be found by almost any fourth grader and should they find something "juicy" you can bet it will be all over school.

Student Issues

Anger Management, Students and Yourself!

The best advice I have goes back to that *emotional detachment* I wrote of earlier. If you understand that students are "disabled" in their ability to comply and follow through, and that it is generally not a premeditated act, you can separate the behavior from the person. Even if it is premeditated, that is still an indication of a lack of maturity, part of what defines a child as a child.

As soon as you take it personally, you have lost and need to step back and collect yourself. I recommend that you seek out information about the cognitive development of children and teenagers. It's fascinating and makes me wonder how any education can happen at all, but the fact is, it does.

The pay-off is that you do not become emotionally charged when this behavior confronts you, the student in turn will calm down and is more likely to comply. If tension is building, have them express why they feel the way they do and spend your time listening.

When they finish, ask, "Can I give you some of my thoughts on this?" If they say no, then fine, they have made that choice. If they say yes, it is an opportunity for them to grow and shows you they are open. Even if the child says no, later they may begin to open up.

Before offering advice though, repeat what you understand from their conversation with you. Reiterate the key points and see if they agree that you fully understand. This is modeling good conversational behavior with them. If they give you information that may be alarming, it is important that you remain calm and detached so they can continue to share and be listened to. When both are clear about the information you can offer your advice and they will listen more intently as they know now you have listened.

It is also okay to say you don't know, or that you will find out and get back to them, or that you need to seek the help of a professional. If they are telling you about an abusive issue, drugs, or criminal behavior, you need to speak to guidance and possibly an administrator. It is important that you do not keep it to yourself or you will be in a position of serious liability. If you report information that it turns out was not true or inaccurate you will be protected by law. You were acting out of the best interest of the child. The only problem you would face is if you reported knowingly false information with malicious intent. It is the only thing that can hurt you legally and that is a very high standard for a lawyer to prove.

The Noncompliant Student

There are levels of noncompliance. It can be in little things like staying in their seats, or can be larger if they simply choose not to work and larger still if this nonparticipation continues. (I also check to see if they are classified students with special accommodations I am required to meet.)

My first approach is to name the behavior and ask for it to stop. Sometimes I can use humor here as well. "Johnny, can you hear that? Your seat is calling for you, it's lonely." Slowly I escalate as necessary. Some kids after all only need a reminder. There is no need to use a sledgehammer when a tack will do. Overreaction shows you to be unreasonable, arbitrary, and unfair. Students will start to lose respect for you.

If a reminder is not working I seek out additional information to find out why they are not complying. Maybe their seat is dirty or wet? I don't know until I ask. Sometimes I need to take them to the hallway and address the issue with a longer "I" statement. "I really need you to stay in your seat. You're a really popular guy and when you wander, the kids do less work because you are sometimes more fun than the work, but I need to be sure everyone has the opportunity to do the best they can. Can you help me out here?" Maybe allow him to wander for the last minute of class if he has been productive. Be sure to give him a little post-it note saying "Thank you for staying in your seat, I really appreciate it." You need to balance your discipline with praise.

If you dish out criticism once, praise twice. I try to end the class with some overall praise and individual observations.

Document All You Can

When issues arise, it may be a good idea to keep a professional journal to document these instances with tiny notes. This way if there is a pattern of behavior, you may be able to address it better.

When giving detentions or office referrals you will need a clear paper trail. This limits your liability and makes it easier to document patterns of behavior. Be especially sure to pay closer attention to your students that legally require additional accommodations. If you have the ability to set up a bulk email to stay in contact with these parents, it will be helpful. You can shoot them emails about upcoming deadlines so they can cover material at home. Even if they do not, you will be covered because you now have evidence that you have in fact, made parent communication important for these children.

Always remember that legal accommodations must be followed and that you are held liable if you do not. You can lose your job and certification.

Documentation can help avoid future problems. This would involve the days you need to be out. If you are sick, really sick, I would encourage you to visit your doctor and get a note, especially non-tenured staff so you have proof, via a note from a physician that you were legitimately ill. This will be part of what they consider when looking at you for tenure. Attendance can be a big issue.

Though your supervisors may understand your need to take a day off, they may not be the persons who ultimately decide if you stay or go. It might be a superintendant you have never met. This documentation will be important for them regardless if your supervisor says, "Don't worry about it."

Communicating with Parents

You may become friends with some parents; some may already be friends if you live near or in your own district. It is important to keep a professional distance from them. If some communication from a parent seems angry or unreasonable, ALWAYS make your supervisor aware of it. They may confirm that the person you are dealing with has a history of being difficult. They may also offer you advice for responses. It may be prudent to have your supervisor review your response before you send it, to be sure you are not opening yourself to larger issues.

These communications should be spell checked, re-read and re-thought before you send it. If it contains emotional adjectives, consider making them more clinical. A nonemotional response to parents is often wise and will help deflate some circumstances. Consider the tone of words you use. If Johnny lied to his parents about what happened in the room, you might want to avoid calling their precious Johnny a "liar." Instead speak to his assertions as inaccurate or that he was mistaken. The words you choose can have real impact on how that parent will respond to you. My tip is that you answer the email as if it is how you would respond to your principal should he or she be writing you. Be respectful and honest.

Personally I create a folder in my email for ALL parental contacts so it is all in one place. This helps me stay on top of issues and I can quickly update specific parents about issues that arise. You want parents to become your advocate, not your nemesis.

Consider too that students are generally a diverse group. While some may live in nice homes, even rich schools have poor kids. Their may be kids who are wards of the state or living with relatives who are not focused on that child's achievement. They may be struggling just to find a job, kick addictions, or be in the middle of doing so. Never make assumptions about your students based on your own life's experiences. You have to assume there are larger issues, outside of school, that may be affecting their achievement or lack of it.

I-Pods and Cell Phones

First and foremost you need to be in compliance with school policy on these issues. If the rules say no cell phones and listening devices, then that is the policy and you are contracted to follow. If a few people are lax, then there is no consistency for the kids. Even if those around you are not following through, you need to cover your own butt and be sure you are in compliance.

That said, there are reasonable ways to include music in your room. If you have an I-pod dock, maybe you can allow students to play their mix for the class while people quietly work? I do for my students but I also add that if one curse pops up, it is banned and they will be written up. I ask that the music be relatively mellow too.

If a student says they need to call a parent, direct them to the office. It is the appropriate place for phone calls to be placed.

Whatever you do, be very clear with students about these expectations and follow through with consequences. If you do not, they only learn that your rules are flexible and that they need not always comply.

Dealing with Unstable Personalities

Okay, I realize this is politically incorrect, but we have all met people that belong in this category. There are some people who are simply not reasonable, argumentative without cause, and not completely in touch with reality. We deal with a diverse population; rich, and poor, educated and not, healthy and addicted, productive and incarcerated. Some of our most difficult students come from very trying home environments.

This is where documentation will be your best friend. You may find yourself in a situation where you have to defend yourself. It is also why you should share unusual communication from parents with a supervisor. I would guess this happens, even in small ways annually. Luckily I have only had to deal with a small handful of truly difficult situations, but all were difficult, one traumatic, and made me doubt my career choice.

Students are still forming their sense of self. They are still malleable to some degree. Your example of professionalism may inspire them to seek a way out of their difficult situation. Your perseverance may have ramifications far beyond what you anticipate. If you are lucky enough, you may hear again from this student later that you have helped save them from their own poor choices. These positives outweigh the negatives.

The reality is that these unstable people are rare and need to be seen for what they are, a rarity that you will encounter. Check with guidance counselors and/or the school psychologists for help. Helping you deal with these situations is part of their role in the school.

Special Needs Students and Aides

It is worthy of reiteration here that you must meet the guidelines of the accommodations required for your special needs students (504 plan or I.E.P.) If you are not in compliance, then you put your job and teaching certificate in possible jeopardy.

Personally I feel that too many students are assessed 504 plans. Some parents pester their pediatrician till they get a diagnosis of ADD or ADHD etc., often without the advice of a therapist or psychologist. A plan is created and teachers are required to comply. Even as I write this, a student with little difficulty has been given a plan and all that it requires is that the student emails me for missed assignments. Any student can email any teacher for this, but now it's in a written legal document, a testament to waste of school resources. Be that as it may, I need to have this paperwork on file and report back if a student does not email me for missing work—one more thing to add to my heap of work.

Some students are designated an aide most likely because they have a physical disorder or are severely impaired in other ways. If a students is assigned an aide, and that aide is required to be there, be very cautious about allowing that child in your room without the aide. If they are, make note of and report that irregularity. You do not want a child with a sever seizure disorder to be without an aide. We have one student in our school where the aide is provided a magnet to restart the child's heart if a seizure becomes too severe. The liability is obvious and you need to be aware of these situations and proactive if there are irregularities. Remember, too, not to confront that student about these issues.

Aides too can be a classroom resource. Communicate with them, understand their role with that student. Are they open to helping with the class or do they prefer to be observational? I would check too with guidance to confirm officially what their role is, to be sure you are not taken advantage of nor are they. Some like to help with attendance or passing out supplies or helping others in class, they may be bored if their only role is to supply that magnet on a rare occasion. Though obviously necessary, they may want to be more involved in your classroom.

When testing students with 504/IEP plans, be sure you follow accommodations to the letter. You may find it helpful to make a special alternative test for these students or have them take their test with someone in guidance for one-on-one attention. This is often helpful. I often use a Scantron format test, where students fill in bubbles and I run the answer sheets through a machine. I always make a write-in version of this test so those with difficulty gridding bubbles can just write in the answers. I make this available to my 504/IEP students but also my non-classified students too.

Guidance from Guidance

Your guidance department can be your best advocate. This is where you can get additional information about your classified students, learn about their backgrounds, or issues that they face. Privacy laws may prevent them from emailing you details, but a one-on-one sit-down conversation may help you in understanding why a difficult student is difficult and ultimately help that student succeed.

These are the same people you need to contact if there are difficulties you observe. Changes in behavior, kids sleeping in class, change of attitude, change of dress... all might be potential indicators of larger issues, some may even indicate suicidal thoughts. In some cases, if you do not report these observed changes you may be liable should something happen. Don't write off behavioral changes as kids being kids, report these and your concerns and let the professionals have a look. Most schools have a procedure outlined for such things and may provide in-service programs about it as well.

Breaking up Fights

Know your school's policy and how they expect you to react. Again, there may be a procedure in place. MOST places though forbid physical teacher intervention. Teachers have been fired for doing so. Touching a child, even to protect another may put you in a liable position. What if the student was

punched by the other while looking away and they assume you did it? You might be their target and this has happened.

A colleague of mine tried to break up a fight and got student blood on himself. It was a nightmare! For privacy reasons asking about their hepatitis or HIV status cannot be revealed. He had to go to a clinic for evaluation. The school would not pay for Hepatitis B vaccinations until a grievance was filed, and now he has the "so be it" attitude when he sees a fight.

You may be covered by some "Good Samaritan" laws, but not always. Policies generally demand that you simply call administration or a school's officer should you have one. Move people away, demand that they stop, possibly position yourself, if you can, to make the fight stop. There is little you should do other than what is required.

You may ask yourself a page full of "what-ifs" as I did, but every situation is different and you need to do what you can and what is expected by your district policies.

If at all possible take note of all witnesses in the area. Maybe use your cell phone to take a picture if they are kids you do not know, and let administration sort it out. Personally I feel that the observers that are "cheerleaders" of a fight should be equally culpable, as they have encouraged it to continue, but that's a separate issue.

Documentation is key here too. Most districts will have a form to fill out where you report all you saw and observed and any witnesses to the incident. You may have to fill out a report too for the nurse about any injuries that happened.

Every school is different. I find those with consistent rules and enforcement have fewer problems than districts where discipline is arbitrary or heavy-handed.

Bloodborne Pathogens, Health Issues, and Immunization

For the reasons I point out in the previous section, and our diverse populations, you are potentially exposed to communicable diseases. This year I caught mycoplasma pneumonia also known as "walking pneumonia." After being sick for 6 weeks and getting a wrong diagnosis, and wrong antibiotics, I was referred to a specialist who made the diagnosis, even after having a negative chest x-ray. It took him all of 5 minutes based on my symptoms and asked, "do you teach school?" It turns out this little gem does not usually effect children as harshly but in adults, can be a real problem. Worse, your body cannot build immunity to it so you can get it again and again in one season.

First year teachers are prone to some of the worst exposures. They have not yet built up immunity to the common illnesses we encounter in schools. You should be proactive, get all your immunizations, take your vitamins, wash your hands often. I even keep a spray bottle of rubbing alcohol on my desk and spray my lavatory passes and door handles from time to time.

Most districts begin the year with training about bloodborne pathogens and what to do if there is a potential risk of exposure. Students with HIV and hepatitis do not have to reveal their status, so you must assume and react that every exposure may contain these and other diseases. Generally your custodians are certified to clean up such issues and you should report blood or body fluid—like spit—exposure immediately. If you get sick from exposure at school and do not report it, you may be on your own and unable to apply for worker's compensation or the health benefits that accompany it.

There is a wealth of information about all of this, enough possibly to scare you, but seek out the school's nurses. They most likely have literature to help you understand procedures and risks in the school environment. If you do not have a school nurse, check with your local clinic or family doctor.

Professional Issues

Administration: Getting Called to the Principal's Office is Still Scary

Your administrators can be your advocates or your nemeses. Though you do not want to "kiss butt," it is important to build a good working relationship with them. Often administrators were once teachers but felt the need to advance and help a greater number of students or mold the learning environment. Some veteran teachers may chuckle at this idea, but I believe it to be true, and I considered it myself for a time, but I like what I do and feel I am good at it.

You need to share and share often with your administrator. If you do not have tenure, this needs to be deliberate, as your status depends on their approval or disapproval. They can help you deal with a difficult parent. Ultimately if they are happy with your performance and a parent is not, the administrative opinion will outweigh the parent.

Non-tenured teachers should make a point of inviting administrators to their room. Maybe paper invitations to show off a particularly good lesson, something that points to you being a "team player" or following their new focus of the year, or school/department goal. Send them little press releases about your content area or achievements you have outside of the classroom.

Your goal is to have them on your side and that may mean pushing yourself a bit. Just as there can be good and bad teachers, the same can be said for administrators. Some may ask too much of you, some may be too hands-off, and make you feel alone. If you feel something is amiss, send copies of emails and correspondence to your union representative, and talk to your colleagues. They may have some advice for you.

If you feel that there is a serious issue afoot, you need to speak to your union. They will know the laws that apply and what should be done. They are generally pretty good about understanding the tightrope you walk and can offer advice or a lawyer should you need one.

I am a firm believer in the power and necessity of a good union. Not all administrators may have the student's or your best interest at heart.

Professional Development

This comes in several forms. Sometimes these meetings are held within the school, when students are on a vacation, sometimes this is at programs at conferences or outside venues, sometimes this is on your own and may be with or without credit. All forms of professional development should be noted in your annual report, copies sent to your advisor, and noted in your professional file.

New laws state that you need to be doing a certain number of professional development hours every few years. In New Jersey we need to have certificates that prove 100 hours of additional training every five years.

I wish I could say that the in-house in-service training is the best, but often it is the lowest common denominator. It provides an opportunity for everyone to meet the state and federal requirements. It sometimes provides important information on things like bloodborne pathogens and evacuation drills, but this is annual, and after 20 years, I find myself snoozing during some of this. I feel the most valuable thing that teachers can do is meet interdepartmentally, share best practices, and find ways to bring content across the curriculum—sadly, this is rare.

Whatever your feelings, in-house in-service is required and should you take off, you might be docked pay. It is generally the easiest of days to attend, you're paid to be there, and expected to be there. Every one that I have attended required a check-in so that attendance was verified.

Observations

These can be a bit unnerving but are a necessary part of administrators seeing if you are doing what they expect of you. I would invite you to speak to a colleague to do an observation of you early and help identify any areas of weakness that an administrator may spot.

You should also look at the evaluation form to know what key things will be observed or expected. Generally they want to see:

- You have strong classroom management policies
- You are following attendance procedures
- You are using differentiated forms of instruction and evaluation
- You engaging the students appropriately
- You have good content that relates to the student's experience
- You have a solid closure activity that wraps up the "big ideas" of that day's lessons.

Make a script or outline, refer to your notes, do not rush, be flexible, let the kids know that they may be part of the observation. Do not openly threaten them or offer rewards; I guarantee it will get back to your observer and not be looked upon as favorable. There are no secrets in education and information flows instantly with cell phones. "Mr. So-and-so gave us cookies for being good yesterday!"

Even after 20 years in the classroom, I still make some notes to be sure I hit all the key points that are expected. You're never too old or experienced to look good for the boss.

PIP/APR

The PIP (Professional Improvement Plan) or APR (Annual Progress Report) is generally done at the end of the year. It is a review of your job and critical for non-tenured employees. This is where you will need to cite your professional development hours, special things you have done in your classroom and outside of the classroom that relate to your job.

I keep a journal on my computer desktop and add things as the year progresses. By the time the end of the year is upon me, it may be easy to forget a collaboration you did, or something you helped with or attended. You should document anything that will help them see you are an invaluable resource and a team player.

New teachers should consult with a veteran teacher as a mentor and go over the forms before submitting them. They will be able to help you fine-tune it to put yourself in the best light and avoid innocent things that can be taken out of context if not clear.

Some districts unofficially require that some "area of improvement" needs to be included. One can argue that everyone can improve, but this unwritten policy seems a bit unfair unless you, as the teacher, have input into what area you would like to focus on. That said, there may be nothing you can really do about it.

If there is a negative comment in your PIP/APR, see a union representative before responding. In many cases you can add a rebuttal to a negative comment that must be kept with the report. This will help clarify the issue should you seek employment elsewhere and they have questions about your review.

Curriculum work / Specificity vs Broad

When writing curriculum, you should keep in mind that whatever you put in it is then LAW until it is reviewed and rewritten. If you include that a specific topic that must be covered in a specific way, you are stuck with it. This can sometimes be for as long as a decade or more in some places. It may be better to include a statement about "suggested activities" and make a short list.

When I write curriculum, I try to be as broad as possible so that I know I will have the most flexibility to cover the material in a way that will most engage my students. I include topics that all my students should have an understanding of when they leave my class. I am careful to edit this, so as not to cover too much. Though I always do more than is required by my curriculum, the person coming after me may not. You need to set a fair level of information that the student must know.

Curriculum does not just come out of your head. There are state and federal guidelines and mandates you must include. You will have older copies to review or if it is a new content area, you can certainly use the internet as a resource to find what other schools are doing. It is a good idea to do a bit of research and see what schools are top rated for your area. Request a copy of their curricula and integrate them into the one you must create.

In many cases you are paid a per diem rate for this work as it is considered outside your normal workday, unless your union's contract says different. Many times this takes place during the first few weeks after school closes. If you are asked to do the work for free, ask the union about this.

Committees and Volunteering

This is a must for non-tenured teachers. You need to show the school that you are a valuable resource and team player. This is sometimes paid work, but often not. If you feel it is excessive, you should speak to your union, but in most cases it's a few additional hours a week.

Consider helping with something you already enjoy or suggesting a new club. Coaching can be very rewarding and help you make connections to the community. They will be the ones to support you if things get politically rough.

Don't forget to "toot your horn" if your club or activity does something special, like community support or some outreach program. Press releases with photos often run in local newspapers or school websites. Be sure to cast some light onto your school and credit any administrator who may have been a part of it. The more you look good, the more they look good.

Additional Paid Positions

If you need to add to your income, check with your Board of Education office and see if there are any additional paid positions available. Some schools need teachers for home instruction. Sometimes coaching positions pay very well and someone can need a replacement at the last minute.

Class coverage also usually pays too. This is when the school cannot find enough substitute teachers and they ask you to cover a class when you should have a period off. You may be paid a small set fee, but it adds up. Find out who coordinates the substitute teachers and see if it an option. Our school has a form that goes around and we reply with the periods we are available should they need a substitute.

After school hours for detentions can be paid too, though it's a rough bunch sometimes. If you manage it well and mandate a quiet study environment, this can be a good time to stay on top of paperwork.

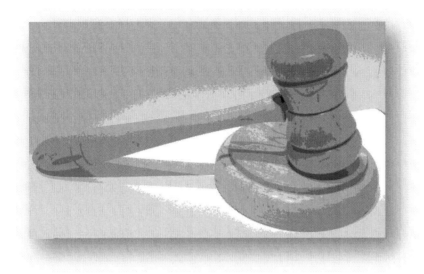

Legal Issues

504 plans and IEP's (Accommodations)

You will be given or need to get the 504/IEP plans for your students. You should also be aware who is on the 504 committee. Because of privacy laws, you may not know who they are until you are told by guidance. You need to review the accommodations you need to make and be sure you follow these guidelines. If you do not, you can lose your job, and possibly your certificate to teach.

Because of privacy concerns, you are not allowed to highlight these kid's names on your attendance, as it identifies them to others and breaks privacy laws. You will need to find a creative way to keep these kids in mind. If they fall through the cracks, miss work, or fail, you need to have clear back-up to show you did everything you could to ensure that they had every opportunity given to them, and that you have been in communication with guidance, your immediate administrator and their parents/guardian.

DO NOT communicate problems to parents without copying all communication with guidance and administration, you may even ask them to communicate for you. What you write and say, if not in compliance with the plan, can put you in a liable position. Never act as an island.

Privacy Issues (What You Can Say to Students)

Privacy is a big issue in the school system. You are given little, if any background about your students. This means you need to remain flexible and able to adjust to new information.

You will not know who may have a communicable disease, so you need to treat them all as if they have one. You won't know who is poor or rich, who is suicidal, who has a drug history, whose father passed away or is in jail or being deployed to a warzone, unless the parent or the child tells you. You need to know all these populations are under your care.

This can be a small positive in that you start off without preconceptions of your classes and each year is new. It means students do not have to be burdened by baggage from the previous year, so it is a fresh start for them. As students mature, some who were very difficult mature into great workers. The reverse can happen too when hormones kick-in. Often I hear in the faculty room, "You have Johnny? He's a real handful, last year he _____." My reply is often that they have not been a problem at all for me. This may be because of my subject, or how I handle my students, but it may be that over the summer, Johnny got an ADHD diagnosis and some medication to help his behavior and you will be unaware of it.

This privacy barrier means you are outside the information loop. You won't know many things that might change your approach to a student. You need to be alert to changes in their patterns of behavior and be willing to ask some questions and seek some advice if an issue comes to light that you think is larger than the student should handle alone.

Personally, I will not even call out grades for quizzes. I think that breaks the privacy issue and potentially the trust of your students. If they want to know their grade, they need to get up, come to me, and see their paper. If they share it afterword, so be it, it was their choice. Even if they tell me, "Just say it," I refuse. Ultimately if you allow grades to be called out, those who prefer it remain private may be embarrassed or shy because of classmate pressure or competition. You need to be sensitive to this.

Reporting Dangers (Suicide, Drugs, Abuse, Other)

As a teacher you may become privy to important information. You are often the first layer of defense for both your students and the school. You need to know what should be passed on and who to pass it to. Your first source should generally be your supervisors. If something of an emergency arises, and you feel the need to "go over their head," make sure you keep them in the information loop, otherwise your administrator may become less than friendly.

You may overhear conversations, and though it sometimes may be bragging and may not be truthful, you should report things you hear about drug and alcohol use. Imagine if you didn't and the next week that same child is killed for driving under the influence. Sadly, these things happen daily across the country.

There are two categories of issues; ones that are happening now, and others that may have already happened or may happen. For the latter, most schools have a resource officer to refer "students at risk."

If you suspect a student is "under the influence" while under your care, you may have a different person you need to inform, usually a principal, and it may involve police action. As a teacher, even if you only suspect that a student may be currently under the influence of alcohol or drugs, you are bound by law to report it, and you are fully protected in doing so. Administration will do all they can to keep your name private, but if something goes to court, your name may be revealed but you cannot be liable even if your report or suspicion is incorrect. You are the referrer, and what happens after that is not in your hands. The professionals evaluate, make determinations, and follow through. It can sometimes be a simple thing, like they forgot to take their ADHD medication or had too much, but this is NOT for you to determine, your role is to refer.

This is the same if you overhear or become aware of or suspect issues of sexual or physical abuse, suicidal references, changes in behavior, sleeping often in class, or acting very differently than usual. Your school may have a referral form for you to check off your observations and help you make the decision to refer or not to. When in doubt, refer.

The ONLY way you can be liable is if you reported a child because you purposefully wanted to make his or her life difficult. This also has to be proven in a court of law and to prove malicious intent is extremely difficult. Because teachers pass an FBI background check, and references are scrutinized rather thoroughly, this is a very rare issue. The law tends to side with the teachers as certified professionals.

Bias Language and Bullying

Fag, homo, gay, ni**er, fatty, etc, are all examples of bias language. The federal laws state that all public institutions must be free from any discrimination based on race, color, religion, sex, or national origin. Any statement said to degrade these protected classes within a school, including sexuality, is considered a bias crime. This goes a bit further in schools now and includes any kind of bullying for those outside these groups. So if a student makes fun of another student's clothing, it is bullying and in some states, a bias crime.

The laws are in flux, and moving in the direction of zero tolerance for bullying and biased language. You as the teacher are charged with stopping it and reporting it. If two boys are chatting about a sexual encounter they had with a girl last weekend, and it is overheard by other students who feel uncomfortable about it, they might not tell you. They may however tell their parents who will in turn tell the administrations, and you are called to the office with union representation to be told your employment is under review.

If they can show a pattern of you not addressing biased language or bullying YOU can be charged with that crime, as you are the adult who allowed it, and created a pervasive atmosphere of bias. If your school does not take action, that parent may be able to sue the school, the Board of Education, and your name will be on the top of that list.

"Boys will be boys," is not acceptable and the straightest path to unemployment. You must address these issues as they arise. You need to make it clear that this behavior will always be referred upward. There is no room for interpretation, let administration take that on. Your classroom needs to be a bias free zone.

Some are quick to "blame the parents" for bias behavior, but some bullying, like for kids whom are perceived to be gay, may be because the bully, has questions about their own sexuality and are acting out to suppress their own fears. Consider this too when making referrals for behavior incidents.

Teen Suicide

Suicide is between the 7th and 10th leading cause of death among teenagers. It is much higher for LGBT (Lesbian, Gay, Bisexual, Transgendered) students and questioning youth (those not sure)—sometimes as high as 50%—consider suicide as an option, and they are two to three times more likely to commit suicide over their heterosexual peers.

If your room is not bias free, you exacerbate their stress and thoughts of suicide by not stopping biased language. Consider that 10 to 15% of students may be silently LGBT, and one kid calls another "a homo," in a class of 30 students; three to five will be present for this bias crime. Though boys are more likely to be successful in suicide, girls make attempts at higher rates. Even different ethnic groups have varying rates of suicide, but it is a serious issue. Even the death of a fellow classmate (suicide or not) can be a risk factor for suicide in your school.

Help is available 24 hours a day, every day: 1-800-273-TALK (8255). For gay and questioning youth, 1-866-4-U-TREVOR is a good resource for help and information.

Your school should provide in-service training on this topic but if not, there are good resources available. One I found helpful was at http://spts.pldm.com. It is also a program where you can earn a certificate for the training that will count toward your hours of professional development.

As with all issues like these, you cannot keep this information to yourself. You must follow through and contact the appropriate person in your school to get that student the assistance they need. You are not a certified therapist or psychologist; do not attempt to become the therapist the child really needs. You put yourself in liability if you do.

Videos and Recording in the Classroom

There are a few different ways to view this topic, watching videos, making videos, and some liability issues you should be aware of.

You can record broadcasts to show to students for educational purposes. There are specific laws to cover this, but for the most part, if it advances your student's knowledge and it is not for profit, it is OK. If in doubt, check with the school librarian, who will probably be most familiar with the laws in this area. You could not however show a movie and charge admission for a school event. The makers of the movie and owners need to give permission and be paid a portion of the profits.

If you wish to video or audio tape students, check first with school policy. If the recording is for instructional purposes, it is usually fine, but if is to document the behavior of students, it may be illegal. Any recording without the person's permission puts you in a liable position.

If you use student work for examples, get a release form signed for permission from the parents. If you document work for your own professional portfolio, it is good practice not to photograph students' faces without permission.

The more dangerous thing is students video taping or taking pictures of you. You have no control of what they will do with these images. With digital technology they can alter images, add your head to another body, augment your video so you appear to say things you did not... There is a long list of issues you do not want to become a part of. Even an innocent picture of you in a student's Facebook page may seem fine but what if it is followed by images of that student smoking marijuana or drinking alcohol? The tone of your image becomes dubious. Think of yourself as the next big hit on YouTube.

I DO NOT allow students to take pictures or video of me. Period.

The last thing and most serious, is students taking images of each other. Students are an unpredictable bunch, and sometimes take pictures of people in compromising positions or worse. They do not understand that the transmission of a nude image of one of their peers is in direct violation of law and considered child pornography. It may be done as a joke between friends or with more malicious intent (like to humiliate someone they do not like) but the fact remains, it happens. If one of these images is sent, it is distribution of child pornography. If it appears on your phone, it is possession of child pornography. CRIMINAL.

How could you get such an image? If you share your cell phone information with a student (common for coaches to do). They can take a picture and send to all of their contacts. This is scary stuff; you have no control over it, but you can be prudent in how you share your information. You need to report this information to authorities as soon as possible. If they find out you did not, you will be in deeper trouble. Tracking the sending of such images is VERY easy to do by authorities. They will find out.

If I must share my number, like for a fieldtrip to New York, where I may lose a child, I give them my number on a slip of paper and collect their information as well. I warn them NOT to add my number to their phones and use it only in an emergency.

Gender Issues

One issue here is dress code. I said before, I alert the office as to a female student's dress-code violation. I would never confront them about it. I just opt out and pass the buck. For male students I can just tell them to go and change a shirt or whatever.

You also need to consider if you are being gender fair/neutral in your class. Some teachers unknowingly ask more questions of their male students than female or vice-versa. Try to look at your own patterns of behavior in this regard and adjust accordingly. Maybe checking off names from attendance will give you an idea of where you stand.

You need to look at your behavior toward students and be sure not to make remarks that pertain to gender. Coaches have been known jokingly to address their male athletes as "ladies." We often joke in the classroom, but if most of your joking is aimed at one gender or another, it may become an unhealthy environment, and if documented by an unhappy student, may turn into a lawsuit. Jokes that pertain to gender or sexuality brush up against biased language, and may put you in liability.

New teachers in a high school can often be just 4 to 6 years older than their students. It is important to distinguish yourself separate from the student population by dress or demeanor. Keep your distance emotionally and personally. Do not make comments to other staff or students about a student's appearance (like how pretty or handsome they are). It just opens a window that should remain tightly shut, locked, barred, and sealed. You will become the next hot topic of the faculty room, followed shortly by an interview with administration or authorities.

Politics and Religion

Unless politics or religion is in your content area, these topics should be avoided in personal discussions with students or staff. Obviously when elections happen, their will be discussions. You need to be clear NOT to share your political opinion of who should vote for whom. As a teacher, you are considered an influential person in their lives. If you try to convince an 18-year old student the value of voting democratic over their registered republican family, you will not only be upsetting a family, but possibly be in violation of law.

To speak about politics in an abstract way, relaying facts or news or history is fine, but to say "You should _____ " is a gateway to problems. Coming between a family's values and their children is extremely risky and unwise. We can present information, facts, news, but we cannot tell them what to do in regard to values issues.

For an extreme example, you could have a student who comes from a very racist family. Certainly they are not allowed to express these opinions in the classroom as it is a bias crime. You can curb that behavior, you can present facts and information that may help shape their opinion, but ultimately their family has a right to think however they want to, as long as they do not impede the freedom of others. Your modeling this behavior, of acceptance and tolerance, may help them see a path toward a more enlightened way of thinking.

If you witness any behavior that demeans someone's right to political, personal, or religious freedom, you need to address it immediately, stop it, and refer such behavior to the administration. It is a bias crime, failure to address it means you have supported it and may be guilty as well.

Social Networks, Alias, Student Communication

I have touched on this a bit before but it comes down to remaining separate personally and socially from your students as best you can. Many schools forbid teachers from having Facebook pages or profile online. They are avenues of communication that open you and your school potentially to inappropriate lines of communication. Some may argue that any communication outside of school is inappropriate; I tend to agree for 98% of the time. The other 2% come with parental permission, and may involve a student you mentor or are helping via their family, and all communication is shared with them. Social interactions with students puts you in a bad position and without the protection of school resources or that of your union.

If you choose to still be online socially, DO NOT uses your real name, create an alias and set your controls so that only those 18 and older may see your profile. Do not "friend" students. Keep in mind though that students are rather technologically proficient. They may still be able to find your profile under that different name. With an email address and the right searches, your profile, images, personal ads, and more can be found, copied, and circulated. If you email a student, they will have your IP address and with that they can find a whole lot more about you. Nothing is ever truly erased from the internet. It is all accessible if you know how. Every keystroke, every image, every embarrassing thing you posted is available to those who know how to access the information.

Never share your personal email with students. Your school address is the safest route to communication. There everything is documented to be seen in the light of day. Communicating with students via personal email puts you in potential risk.

The "No Touch" Rule

Unless you are a gymnastics coach, or PE teacher, where physicality is part of the content, DO NOT TOUCH YOUR STUDENTS, nor should you allow them to touch each other. This second part is nearly impossible as kids socially hug, grab, slap, and hose-around with each other all day. You need to minimize it as much as possible.

All a student needs to say is, he or she "touched me and made me feel uncomfortable." That's it, game over. You will have an administrative meeting and more. You will be made to feel uncomfortable, your practices will be questioned, and if it is not the first time, or it could be interpreted to be inappropriate and actions may be taken against you.

When I was in training as a student teacher, I was told it is a good thing to put your hand on a student's shoulder and make a personal connection. That they would listen more and focus more on what you were saying. This is not true in today's litigious world. My advice is, just don't do it.

NEVER be Alone with a Student

By now you may think me paranoid but in my 20 years in the classroom I have seen the good, the bad, and the ugly, as well as the great, the amazing, and the inspirational. Luckily the good things far outweigh the bad.

It is rare, but on some occasions you may be saddled with a student that is overly needy or has a history of not being in touch with reality. In years past, I had been told, "Never be alone with _____, always stand in the hallway if they are the last to leave." They would not give me additional information, but teachers talk, and I found out that this child had some pretty severe issues to deal with, and was not always truthful to authorities. This student presented a certain liability that required that teachers be cautious not to be alone with him or her. It was preferable to stand in the hall where security cameras could see you, and see them leave. This was not monitored, but if an issue came up, there would be some video back up.

This incident made me look at this issue in a broader sense. Students are immature people who do not always understand the repercussions of their behavior. They do not see that a little lie to avoid trouble may produce larger issues for other people. In general, my advice to teachers is to avoid being alone with students. If you need to offer extra help to one during an off period, consider meeting in a public space, or be near an open door. I NEVER am alone with a student without the door being open and always sit them in clear view of the door.

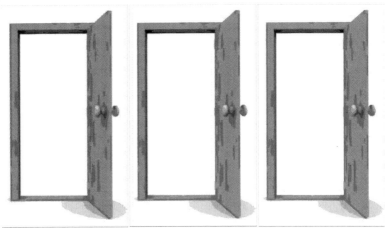

You May be Breaking the Law if _____

- You do not take daily attendance
- You do not stop students from teasing or bullying in your classroom
- You access personal email or make personal calls on school time
- Take school supplies for personal use
- You ignore or allow biased language in your classroom
- You communicate with students outside of school
- You participate in a party with students and alcohol or illegal substances are available
- You tell them how they should vote or pray
- You tell a student that being gay is a sin or somehow wrong
- You do not report suspicious behavior
- You do not report obvious changes in student behavior
- You suspect a student is under the influence of drugs or alcohol and keep it to yourself
- You do not report criminal activity you overhear
- You do not follow the accommodations for classified students
- You video or record students for non-instructional purposes
- You sell something to your students that benefits you financially
- You drive a student home without the knowledge of the district or parents

"Politics"

The Faculty Room

Almost every aspect of school, from students to administration, is discussed in the faculty room. It is generally healthy and appropriate. You can get a reality check from veteran teachers and a perspective from others. We share war stories, and ideas on how to handle certain students, and parents. There is advice about who can be trusted and who to avoid.

As a new teacher I would suggest listening a lot. Even if you do not agree with what is said, you will certainly learn about the tone of your school and colleagues.

It is also wise to keep faculty room chat confidential or people will no longer share or help each other. Though some schools may frown upon faculty room chat, I find it to be important for colleagues to communicate without constraints.

When in Doubt, Be Quiet.

As a new teacher, be cautious of making too many waves or confronting colleagues or administration. It is better to remain proactive and diligent, but every situation is different, and it will take some time to learn what is acceptable, and what is not. You may accidently put yourself in a bad light if you push too hard.

Listen and learn is often the best of policies. Share and see how people react. Learn who is on your side with similar perspectives. They will begin to open up to you and share their observation of "how things are done."

As a new teacher, you may not really be aware of all the backgrounds of the people around you. You could make some offhand comment about the principal, and it might be his child that is a substitute teacher sitting next to you. You might complain about one situation or teacher and the person you are complaining to is his or her life-long friend. I have seen some "foot in mouth" situations occur in the faculty room and it's not pretty.

there may be an occasion when you are asked pointed questions from an administrator that make you feel confused or uncomfortable. If you do feel this way, you can ask for a halt to the meeting and request that a union representative be present. If they refuse, take note of it. It may be best to say nothing more until you have a representative with you no matter your tenure status.

Contract Negotiations

Most schools go through some kind of contract negotiation every few years. If there is good communication between the Board of Education, administration, and teacher's association, these can be relatively smooth, so much so that you may not be aware they are happening.

Sometimes they are anything but smooth The Board of Education seat is often a first step into a life of politics, and sometimes these people want to leave a political imprint so they can advance on to higher offices. Sometimes the relationship between teachers and administration is adversarial. Sometimes financial stresses on a community force unpopular decisions. Sometimes communication is poor and rumors abound. All of these situations may lead to negotiations that can turn very ugly and result in picketing, job actions, and even strikes.

Though you want to be a team player, teachers needs to remain loyal to their union. If non-tenured you may feel unprotected and vulnerable, and by not participating you show yourself to be weak, and an easy target for "the other side." As much as possible, as a non-tenured teacher, you need to take a back seat, but you also need to follow the directions of your union. Your administration and Board of Education know that you are in a difficult position and understand it is just part of the process.

Though some may choose to opt-out of their union, often you must still pay a large percentage of the dues anyway. Union member or not, they have to negotiate your contract and benefits. If you get stuck in a legal situation, the union would cover the lawyer fees in most cases. If you are not in the union, you are on your own. Consider the possibility that administration refuses to pay your increment, or reimburse you for tuition as they promised for some perceived fault that may or may not be true. You have little recourse but your own resources. Even the best of teachers, through no fault of their own, can find themselves in difficult circumstances. Your union can be your advocate.

Whom Do You "Trust?"

There are politics everywhere in a school, among students, teachers, and administrators, all the way to the Board of Education. As a new teacher you will need to navigate and find people you can trust. It is always wise to spend a lot of time listening. If you have a friend already on staff, you may want to ask them with whom they feel they are most comfortable.

Teachers are people: Some gossip and spread rumors; some may leave the room when they hear these kinds of conversations; some will keep your information confidential; some will share it with others as the new "juicy dirt." Some administrators are your advocate; some may be looking for excuses to eliminate staff to meet budget needs. Take your time; watch, look, and listen before sharing confidences.

PTA

Parent Teacher Associations vary in the forms they take. Some are more active, some more supportive, some are more social organizations. Whatever form they take on, you should be aware of their activities and be aware of their political standing within the school.

It is important that you participate if you can or have connection to parents in a professional way. They are your advocates and can support you should issues arise.

Some parent organization offers mini-scholarships and grants. Teachers can apply for mini-grants to buy supplies they cannot normally afford. Most of these organizations are around to be an advocate for the students and ensure they succeed.

"Big Brother IS watching!"

More and more districts are documenting internet access and phone usage.

Consider that if you access your personal email from school, the school's server has access to your accounts, email, passwords, and more. If they wanted to, they can see when you logged on, and if it was during a time you are contracted to be teaching/working/on duty, they can file charges for theft of time, and you can lose your job, and possibly your certificate. (Criminal activity can invalidate your certificate.) Though this is rare, it is not unheard of. Sometimes the relationship between teachers and administration is adversarial, especially during difficult contract negotiations.

Consider too that modern copy machines work off a hard-drive. This can be accessed. If you made copies of a passport for some trip you want to take over a holiday, and you did it on school time because the copier is convenient, it is technically theft of time and materials PLUS someone now has access to your identification! It would be prudent to avoid these things if at all possible or use an office copier, with permission, during off hours. If you have a friendly administrator, ask permission, and it gets you off the hook.

I hate to seem so paranoid about all of this, but it is something the new teacher should be aware of. Some innocent behavior at work is just inappropriate. The safest thing to do is get a phone that can access the internet. This should be the only way to access personal accounts at school. Check too with your phone carrier for teacher discounts. I use Verizon and they offer a 15% discount for teachers in New Jersey. This may be true in other places.

"ABC" Always Be Considerate to Support Staff!

Janitors, secretaries, and other support staff help you do what you do. Remember them at the holiday times and in-between. Take time to say hello, learn their names, chat a bit, and commiserate if you like. They are great people to have on your side and often hear the latest scoop on information before teachers do. They see what's in people's trash and I am sure have some interesting stories. They will also be the ones to tell you when things will be happening in the school that may affect your room, like maintenance, sometimes long before you are told by your supervisor.

Be kind to the lunch ladies, and your portions may increase a bit, or you may end up with a slightly less burnt slice of pizza. They have a tough job and little appreciation for what they do.

Secretaries are the gatekeepers to the school and its functions. Being polite and appreciative in small ways will help processes run more smoothly and accommodations to be met from time to time. Sometimes secretaries are placed in the position of delivering bad news. Remember not to kill the currier. Be sure you separate their job responsibilities from them as a person.

This is not to say you need to bribe people with kindness to make them do their jobs, but these are our colleagues too, and everyone likes to be treated with respect, kindness, and appreciation. It takes little effort and pays off with a happier environment.

Getting and Keeping Your Job

The Reality of Tenure and Non-tenure

Without tenure you can be fired for any reason, and no reason, without explanation. There is no law that says the school needs to supply any grounds for dismissal. It may be they feel you simply do not "fit in" to their style of education, or are not meeting their desired goals for performance. It could be as petty as you said no to putting up a bulletin board, or you were not liked by a peer who was consulted to see if you should be retained or not. Some districts are under heavy budget pinches, so they may not able to retain staff no matter how good they may be. You may never know the true answer as to why, but all non-tenured teachers should keep their options open until they receive notice that they will be on staff for that fourth year. A more pessimistic view would be to wait until you are within the window of notification. (My district must give 60 days notice if they plan not to re-hire you, so I'd wait until 60 days before the opening of school to feel comfortable.)

Tenure generally occurs the first day of your fourth year. There are no trumpets, ribbon cutting, accolades, or handshakes. It is just another day. Your union may do something for you in recognition of the occasion. More often than not, it is just another day and only you know it is special.

So what is tenure? What is the big deal? In a nutshell, it means you cannot be fired without just cause. The school needs to prove that you are unfit to be a teacher. That you have done something illegal or that you were defiant to administration. They need to prove a pattern of non-compliance or negligence. This prevents political firings and arbitrary retribution from an overzealous administrator.

The only exception to this is a RIF notice. "RIF" means **R**eduction **I**n **F**orce. When some schools remove whole departments because of budget failures, tenure is moot. Sometimes they do it for political reasons when a budget fails. They tell the public a program will be cut, and all those teachers get notices that they will not be hired the following year. The community may rally against the cuts, the district says it needs more money, and money is sometimes found, and the teachers reinstated. Welcome to school politics.

There are some legal protections with it. If the position is reinstated, the teacher who lost their job MUST be contacted and offered their position back. They have only ONE CHANCE to say yes or no. If they say no, the position may be given to another person. If they do not offer you the reinstated position, you have legal recourse to sue for your position and lost wages for the time you could have been employed.

A Teaching Portfolio (Createspace.com)

Even though I have been teaching for 20 years, at the time of this book I still document student success in my classroom to prove I am a good teacher and should the time come that I need to seek a job. I have a digital camera in my room at all times to take images as good work happens.

I also like to have students open with an assessment of their skills on the first day, and then track the students with the most improvement for my portfolio, so I can share these successes as needed. This is a concrete way to show my work in the best light for a prospective employer.

This information may also be helpful if the Board of Education seeks to remove departments. It will help you make better arguments to retain your position. Student teachers especially must document as much as possible, as this may be your only time to show your teaching skills in a classroom. I would especially highlight any lessons with an intercurricular approach.

I can also recommend Createspace.com. They are owned by Amazon.com and make "POD" or **P**rint **O**n **D**emand books that then sell on Amazon. There is no fee to use their service except when buying your own books. If you can write a document and save as a PDF file, you can have a book published, and earn royalties. This can make for a nice portfolio, and if in black and white, is very inexpensive. I have a 150 page workbook that costs me less than $3.00 each but sells on Amazon for $24.00.

This can also be a means to become a "published author." This would look impressive on your resume and need not be in your content area. Maybe you have had an idea for a children's story, this can be your opportunity. It is how I have written this book you now hold and is a source of income.

Resume That Looks Like Your Content Area

When I applied for my current job in the early 1990's there were 160 other people applying for the same position. I crafted a resume that that I knew would be very different looking and visually stand out from the others. As much as you may have been told you need to include every piece of information, I am of the belief that the first resume needs to "get you in the door," with bullet points to grab your employer's attention. If you grab them visually, you will be called in for an interview, and you can give them a more detailed traditional resume.

My resume was only one page with two columns. The first column was nearly empty with my contact information at the bottom, the second column was my resume in 9 to 10 point font. These were simple bullet points with my certifications, Praxis exam, experience, and skills, with a small 200-word statement about my teaching philosophy.

The large blank are was where I could add a photo, some visual graphic, some item that would grab them visually, and let them know why I should be considered. I would strongly suggest you look online for images of "creative resumes" and see what others have done. If you have a friend that is good with graphics, maybe he or she can help.

The major thing is that your resume be as creative and distinctive as possible to stand out from the 200 or so other resumes that arrive. You need to start thinking outside the box on this one. How about a resume ON a box with photos inside? How about a treasure map, "Discovering _____ With Mr. Smith," or a cereal box re-designed to market you? These will definitely stand out and get you that first interview.

Why everyone generally sticks to the black and white standard is beyond me in this market.

Parents as Advocates (Letters of Recommendation)

Parents can be your best advocate, especially if you have reached out to them on a regular basis. there may be students you have helped mentor and given additional help to. Keep in contact with these parents as they can be an asset when issues arise. They can speak to the Board of Education or administrators on your behalf. Parents are taxpayers and voters and sometimes have a lot of pull.

I recommend setting up small email lists to keep current parents updated on what is happening in the classroom. Though many schools have web sites to update parents, a personal email from you is more likely to be read. I think this is doubly true of your classified students. I send those families an update before all quizzes and tests and where they can find study-guide information.

If you need to leave a district, either by choice or another reason, you should ask these parents for notes or letters of recommendation. This will show the new district that you keep close contact with families and is usually considered an asset. They know that teachers with a strong connection to parentsand the community can be advocates to pass school budget proposals.

How Soon Administrators Should Know Your Name

In larger schools being recognized can take a long time. You may be a small fish in their large ocean. I highly recommend little notes to administration with a picture that lets them know when you are doing something special in the school beyond normal expectations. Even an invitation now and then can keep you on their radar. There is no need to do too much or become an annoyance, but new teachers need to garner positive attention whenever possible.

Emails may be fine but I feel a little physical note, especially an attractive one, grabs more attention, and makes you look more polished and professional. If they do visit, FOLLOW UP WITH A THANK YOU! This is really key and shows that you value their participation and will be considered when your position is too.

Unions and Contracts

If you are new to teaching you may not understand the importance of your teacher's union. They are the ones to negotiate your salary, set procedures, help you through legal issues, and back you up should you feel something inappropriate is happening professionally. If your school is a "closed shop," it means that everyone pays into the union even if they do not want to be a member. You can refuse membership but may alienate the most powerful advocate to help and protect you. Even if you refuse they will still take a large portion of the dues because of the work they do for all teachers, union and non-union.

I said earlier, consider the possibility that administration refuses to pay your increment or reimburse you for tuition as they promised for some perceived fault that may or may not be true. You have little recourse but your own resources. Even the best of teachers, through no fault of their own, can find themselves in difficult circumstances. Your union can be your advocate.

The contract is your guide to what is expected of you. You need to follow those guidelines, and if there is anything you do not understand, you need to ask your union. If there is something in the contract that you need to be doing, and are not, administration may give you a warning, and start documenting this issue. It can become a reason to end your employment or withhold increment, even if you do have tenure.

You need to also consult your contact if you feel administration is taking advantage of you by asking you to stay after school beyond your required time. Again, you should consult the union when these issues arise. A non-tenured teacher is expected, on some level, to volunteer a bit to show your loyalty to the school, and your willingness to go "above and beyond." A little is not too bad, but I am aware of others asked to put in many hours without reimbursement. If you do not want to fight it, and risk tenure, you should document all this paid time. Make copies of all email or documents stating that they know you are putting in this time. Express the stress but continued compliance with requests. Let your union know. Once you have tenure, you may be able to seek a legal remedy to this unpaid time.

Documentation is key in these situations. Make a folder and keep paper copies of all of this information. Be sure to include headers of all email so there is documented proof of where and when the message was sent.

Promote, Promote, Promote

I highly recommend little notes to administration with a picture that lets them know when you are doing something special in the school outside of normal expectations. Administration though is only one level of communication to promote yourself, your courses, and your department. Consider partnering with others in your department to do a project that will grab larger attention.

Try working with another department to illustrate the interconnectedness of your subjects. Let others know. I would even advise contacting the local press or parent teacher organization to let them know about the special events or projects you do. Anything that brings positive attention to your teaching, your department, or the school in general, is welcome.

When contacting the press, remember to include information about your department leader and that they include the school's name. I have found that if you essentially write a story that you would like to appear in the press, it often runs "as is." I hate to say this, but the local press is generally lazy or overwhelmed. Small staff can mean that the ready-made article is the first to run, especially if it includes photography of the event. They tend to like JPEG images at 300 DPI or PPI resolution. This is an industry printing standard for clear images.

Personal Development and Continuing Education

I outlined the positives and negatives of in-house professional development earlier. These are fine experiences, but you should consider other opportunities. This can take the form of clubs, associations, and college courses. Include this information; it may be helpful for your annual performance review.

If you are able, I recommend continuing work within your content area. In most cases your school will help pay for additional coursework, and your pay increases based on your degree level. The earlier you do this, the more money you will accumulate toward your retirement and bank account.

The additional benefit is that it can give you a feeling of personal satisfaction and a goal outside the classroom to break up the routine. This may not be possible for someone married with small children, but if at all possible, see what you can afford to do.

Use Technology

This may be difficult in the poorer schools with small budgets but anyway you can, try to incorporate technology into your content area when possible and appropriate. Technology itself is a motivator for students. They are familiar with this new "stuff" and see it as fun. It can take the form of internet research or video presentations from YouTube. Students can even make their own.

One of my favorite sites for education information is TED.com. They have some wonderful presentations in all content areas. Though some may be appropriate for your children, many are wonderful for the teacher as well. PBS, National Geographic and the Discovery Channel have an extensive offering of content for the classroom too. There are blogs and other sites that you will find valuable for your content area. Ning has quite a few. Do some searching and bookmark the good ones.

Personal Issues

$aving for Retirement and Investing ASAP

The earlier you start saving, the easier your retirement will be. If you start as a new teacher, you can have more than a million dollars for your retirement. This is NOT an exaggeration.

Here is a short list of things to do:
- Clear your debt in all forms and pay off your credit cards ASAP.
  - Even bankruptcy cannot clear student loan debt.
- Fund a ROTH IRA up to $5000 per year.
  - Invest aggressively early, later adjust it conservatively.
- By 30 years old, if available to you, fund a 403B
  - Split it between fixed income and stock funds.
- Have 8 months of emergency funds in the bank.

Keep in mind, your credit score can actually affect your ability to be hired.

If possible, live UNDER your financial ability. Some lenders will tell you, "You can afford a $250,000 house at your level of income." This figure is usually the upper end of what you can afford, and does not take into account car payments, rising heating bills, etc. Their will always be unexpected financial hardships associated with a home. If they tell you one figure, try to shop at about 50% to 70% of that figure. This may allow you additional funds to create savings and handle emergencies as they arise. If you live like you are poor, you will live comfortably and retire happy.

Find Your Passion Outside School to Avoid Burn-out

It is important to keep yourself fresh and refreshed. Get those 8 hours of sleep. Be good to yourself, but also engage yourself in activities that reinvigorate your, and your creative spirit. Some like to pour themselves into night school, crafts, hobbies, clubs, and social organizations.

In the first chapter, I wrote about loving what you teach. I said for some, taking their subject outside the classroom is beneficial, easily understood when you think of an art teacher painting and exhibiting. A colleague friend of mine teaches math and tells me that the last thing he wants to do is more math when he gets home. Instead he finds that golf and gardening keep him fresh. You may find a woodworking class for a science teacher, may simply allow for creative energies to express themselves and make for a happier person. Some find their bliss in a daily work-out routines, quilting, scrapbooking, painting and exhibiting.

Consider doing something you have always wanted to but never had the time. Many teachers have their summers off and longer holiday vacations. This is a good time to travel, take up a martial art, try a painting class, explore photography, or take a trip through wine country. Do what you need to do to stay fresh and have fun. If you are burnt out, your students will feel it and react accordingly. How can they become excited about a subject that you care little about yourself?

Keeping School Drama Out of Your Home

As a teacher you need to strive to keep work at work. I would recommend not taking work home, but coming in a bit early or staying a bit late to complete this work. In this way, when you go home, you can leave the classroom behind, and focus entirely on your family and home. If I have school work at home, there is a possibility it can be lost. Generally it's sitting there, staring at me, and reminding me of the school day within my sanctuary.

This is not easy for all to do, but I have made the switch myself, and find it very helpful, and in some ways beneficial to my wellbeing. I may share my day a bit with my spouse, but it's a few sentences and not the whole topic of conversation. As best I can, I separate work from home.

This may be a bit difficult if you live in district. You may see students and colleagues on a daily basis. I prefer to live outside my district and I do. Though I still see students from time to time, it is not often, and I feel I can have a private outside life. When in a district, you may become part of the rumor mill in either a positive or negative way. The plus is that you have a vote in what the school does and easy access to advocates when you need them. The lack of privacy though may be too large of a negative.

Dating at Work/"Frenemies"

It happens, and I am sure there are examples of great relationships that started as a collegial friendship. The problem is that if it does not work out, you will have to see the person on a daily basis. You will know them a bit deeper than others and they know you as well. Should a friendship sour, those little personal items can be discussed in places you had hoped they not be shared. I have witnessed this drama and it is not pretty.

You need to weigh these possibilities before beginning a relationship and see if the ramifications are worth it. I tend to be of the mindset that it is better to seek a relationship outside the school. Though it may be more difficult to coordinate vacations, this should not be seen as a negative.

Keep in mind as well that if you decide to go the route of a personal ad, be cautious about using your real name or identifying information such as the subject you teach and for what district. I have said before, students are very internet savvy and can find these profiles with little effort. You need not make it easy for them. Anything they find, you should be sure, will spread like fire through a paper house.

Discrimination and Issues at work

Though rare, issues of sexual harassment can arise as well as other discriminatory issues. You need to be aware of how to report such issues. My best advice is always to contact a union representative who can point you to the relevant information. This is often posted in the main faculty room as well as other legal information about your "Right to Know" in regard to chemicals in the school building. Our room has a poster and information about our civil rights. The school's policies must always comply with federal and state standards.

If someone makes you feel uncomfortable at work for any reason, seek out help. Do not keep it to yourself as such behavior can escalate into something very demeaning. Whenever you are unsure, seek out the advice of a trusted colleague or union representative.

Disclaimer:

There are multiple situations that happen in the classroom that may invalidate some information. Every situation is different. Think of this book as a general guide. Laws and policies change and you should check on anything I provide here with your own district policies and the laws of your state.

NOTES:

NOTES:

NOTES:

NOTES:

NOTES:

NOTES:

NOTES:

NOTES:

NOTES:

NOTES:

NOTES:

If you are an art teacher, you may find my other book helpful.

The Art Student's Workbook in both teacher and student editions.

This workbook was created by a 20-year certified veteran teacher and curriculum writer for classes in drawing, painting and sculpture designed for grades 6 through 12. Lessons are easily adjusted to accommodate special needs students and material availability in many environments from the school classroom to a fine arts camp program. This updated version includes more than 2 years' worth of lesson ideas, project samples, vocabulary, worksheets, sample tests, research paper samples, grading rubrics, sketch and note-taking pages, and short creative 5 minute writing assignments. It is designed to work with Crystal and Davis Publications' materials and the textbook, *The Visual Experience* but may be used alone as well.

This book is also a helpful aid in fulfilling state and federal accommodation requirements (504, IEP) by providing special needs students additional documented and written material that may be taken home. Every lesson is designed to be personal and expressive Fine Art. There are NO "crafty" projects or "cookie-cutter" lessons where everyone has the same outcome.

This book stresses a "Divergent Thinking Processes" approach and creative problem solving, with an art therapy undertone. All lesson suggestions may be done in different media to work within tight budgets. In a time when the economy is strained and schools must choose to make cuts, it is often the art department that is the first to suffer as it is considered peripheral "fluff" or a dumping-ground for students who need a period slot assigned.

Anecdotal evidence from my school's guidance department indicates that students who take my course are 50% LESS likely to fail standardized testing. These are real numbers that can grab the attention of your administration and Board of Education. There is a wealth of evidence that a rigorous arts program benefits students. It may be the inherent problem solving methods we use daily, or our natural "backwards design" approach that helps our students succeed. Art teachers know that these same concepts are simply "what we already do," but are only recently coming into the light as the new "cutting edge" of education.

I feel it is this and something more important.

Art is the one class where the concepts of math, science, history, language, and writing converge in a well-orchestrated, rigorous, and relevant program. We not only come to understand the concepts but we use them and manipulate them for deeper understanding on multiple sensory levels of thinking. Herein I have divided this workbook by multicurricula units so that this concrete connection to academic "core courses" is more easily seen.

Does this mean that an art class loses its creative edge by incorporating other subjects? My twenty-years of experience tells me that this integration enhances it. Students have a deeper understanding of the work, they come to see the relevance, and are more likely to buy into the concept.

When students ask, "Why do we have to know this stuff?" the answer becomes relevant through our daily approach, process, and end products. ALL projects are designed to have successful divergent results, incorporate creative problem solving, and bring relevant connections to students' lives.

This book is built for student success on many levels from gifted to challenged, Which in turn is helpful in fulfilling mandated state and federal accommodations so that no child is left behind.

Please Note: Student copies DO NOT contain lesson suggestions or internet art references.

Order direct from the printer for a discount using code: NXY3Y88L
Teacher's Edition → www.createspace.com/3412518
Student Edition → www.createspace.com/ 3435591
Trade Edition → www.createspace.com/ 3522178

The "Trade Edition" is best for administrative review as it highlights how this art course integrates core content applications.